CATASTROPHIC KINGS

WE WANT A **KING**!

Andy Robb

Catastrophic Kings

Copyright © 2001 John Hunt Publishing Ltd
Text © 2001 Andy Robb
Illustrations © 2001 Andy Robb.
Reprinted 2003

ISBN 1-84298- 045-9

Design by Nautilus Design, UK

Scriptures quoted from the Good News Bible published by The Bible
Societies/HarperCollins Publishers Ltd., UK,
© American Bible Society,1966, 1971, 1976, 1992.

Write to:
John Hunt Publishing Ltd
46A West Street
Alresford
Hampshire
SO24 9AU
UK

The rights of Andy Robb as author and illustrator of this work have been
asserted in accordance with the Copyright, Designs and Patents Act 1988.

A CIP catalogue record for this book is available from the British Library.

Printed by Tien Wah Press Ltd. Singapore

CONTENTS

Introduction

What's the most boring thing you can think of? Okay, now multiply it by a zillion.

That's how boring a lot of people think the Bible is. The funny thing is, most people who think the Bible's mega mind-numbingly boring have never even read it!

Crazy or what?!

Imagine turning down a triple whopper chicken, cheese and yoghurt burger with gherkin and custard relish just because you'd never tried it...

On second thoughts that wasn't such a good suggestion.

But you get my point?

I mean, I'll bet you didn't even know that the Bible's got adverts in it to tell people what's going to happen in the future or that it told people that the world was round thousands of years before we'd worked it out.

There's so much stuff in the Bible we won't be able to look at every bit of it but the bits we've chosen will hopefully make you start to realise that the Bible maybe isn't quite so boring as you thought.

Have fun!

So What's The Bible All About?

The Bible isn't just one whopping great book.

It's actually 66 not-quite-so-whopping great books all whacked together like a sort of mini library.

The first book in the Bible is called Genesis, which was also the name of a pop group your parents once liked but they won't admit to it even if you hang them from the ceiling by their toenails... and the last book is called Revelation which as far as I know wasn't the name of a pop group your parents once liked.

To keep things simple, the Bible is mainly about two things.

God.
And people.

Some interesting questions.

Who exactly wrote the Bible?
People.

Who decided what to write about?
God.

So how did they know what God wanted them to write?
Did God send an e-mail?

Er, not quite.
Here's one way of looking at it.
Imagine two people in love.

Enough of that!
Sorry, have I put you off your lunch?
When people are in love with each other all they want to do is
spend every waking hour gazing lovingly into each other's eyes.
(I know, it's horrible, isn't it!)

The way they hug and cuddle each other you wonder whether they've been permanently super-glued to each other for all eternity.

It even gets to the point where they start to think each other's thoughts.

Well, that's sort of what it was like for the guys who wrote the Bible (without the cuddling bit).

They spent so much time with God that they got to know what he was thinking and what he wanted to say.

Sometimes God even spoke to them in dreams or gave them visions of what he wanted to say.

They were totally in touch with God so that what they wrote was as if God had written it himself.

So what sort of things does God want to say to us?

For starters, the Bible tells us that there is a God and that he made you and me and the whole universe.

It also tells us that he wants us to be his friends and how we can do that.

What good is a book that was written *even before* my mum and dad were born? People might not wear silly costumes like they did in the past but God hasn't changed a bit, so what he had to say to people with funny headdresses and sandals thousands of years ago is still important for us.

This Boring Bible book's all about a whole load of kings and how well (and how badly) they ruled the Israelites.

As well as lots of kings we've thrown in some judges and some prophets as well for good measure but you'll have to read on to find out what *they* did.

All in all the period of history mentioned in *Catastrophic Kings* covers an amazing 34 books of the Bible but they don't all get a mention.

Here are some of the ones we're going to whiz through...

JOSHUA, JUDGES, SAMUEL, KINGS, PSALMS, PROVERBS, ISAIAH, JEREMIAH and DANIEL.

(By the way, I was only joking about hanging your parents upside down by their toenails - nose hairs work much better!!!)

Here's a question for you.

What would you do if you moved house and then, when you got to your new home there were still people living there? Well, that's sort of what happened to the Israelites when they went to live somewhere new and we're about to find out exactly what *they* did about it.

Just in case you're wondering who on earth the Israelites are, let me quickly fill you in.

If you've read any of the previous Boring Bible books (and if you haven't I want to know **why not**!!!), then you'll know all about how God made the whole wide world, oceans, land, trees, animals, creepy crawlies, dinosaurs, smelly pigs...

...in fact anything and everything that there is and then, as the icing on the cake, he popped in a couple of human beings to look after it all.

(That was Adam and Eve, if you must know.)

Adam and Eve, with the help of a not-very-nice snake, disobeyed God just like naughty children do their parents. This was not a good move.

Not only did it break their friendship with God but the beautiful world they lived in started to go bad like a rotten, maggotty apple does.

So, What Would You Do If You Were God?

a Blast Adam and Eve off the face of the earth?
b Have nothing to do with the human race ever again?
c Make a fresh batch of people to replace the first lot?
d Put the dinosaurs in charge of everything instead?
e Give humans a second chance?
f Something else?

If you said e) then you'd be right.
God had made people to be the very top of his creation and to have a very special friendship with him like no other animal or creature could ever have.
There was nothing God wanted more than to patch things up with the human race but first off, God needed to remind them who he was and how much he cared for them.
Introducing Abraham.

God picked out Abraham to start a brand new nation of people who would obey him and love him and who he could use to show the rest of the world that he was *still* there and that he *still* cared for them.

This nation was none other than the **Israelites** but you'd probably worked that out already, hadn't you, smarty pants?

If you want to find out all about how the Israelites got started and some of their early adventures then you're going to have to get your hands on a copy of the Boring Bible book, *Hotchpotch Hebrews*.

But don't worry too much for now.

Our story kicks off where *Magnificent Moses* ended, with the Israelites getting ready to enter the land of Canaan which God had said they could have as somewhere to live.

Unfortunately, their leader, Moses, had died just before they made it but God had now handpicked a *new* main man to take his place.

His name was **Joshua.**

The good news was that Joshua had been with Moses right from the very beginning so he knew exactly what was what.

The Low-Down On Joshua

1 I've been a slave in Egypt just like the rest of the Israelites.

2 I saw God punish Pharaoh and the Egyptians with ten terrifying plagues when he said "No!" to letting us go free.

3 I was there when God miraculously parted the Red Sea so that over two million of us Israelites could cross it.

4 I was there when God fed us with food from nowhere as we wandered through the desert.

5 I was there when Moses went up Mount Sinai to meet God.

6 I was there when most of the Israelites decided that they'd had enough of being God's special nation.

7 I was there when God made us wander round and round the desert for 40 years because of the Israelites' constant grumbling against God.

Okay, Joshua, you've got the job, but first you're gonna have to wait until all those moaners and groaners have died.

There was no place in this new land that God was giving the Israelites for anyone who wasn't prepared to trust him.

At long last, the Israelites were finally ready to say "Goodbye" to the desert...

...and "Hello" to the land of Canaan.

Hang on a minute!
Not so fast.
There's just one itty bitty
problem.

There's already people living there!

Yep, that's right.

God was giving the Israelites the land of Canaan to live in but first there was the small business of getting rid of its inhabitants.

Now, you're probably thinking that it's a bit hard on the people already living in Canaan having to get out so that the *Israelites* can come in and settle there instead, aren't you?

Well, let me fill you in with a bit of stuff about the Canaanites before you start feeling *too* sorry for them.

Everything You Ever Wanted To Know About The Canaanites But Were Afraid To Ask!

The Canaanites (which is what the people of Canaan were called if you hadn't guessed) didn't worship the God that the Israelites worshipped, the God who had made the universe, the world and all its people.

They had their own made-up gods who were nowhere near as nice.

And they didn't just have *one* god. They seemed to have one for every occasion but the three most important ones in their eyes were Baal, Dagon and Astarte.

If you wanted to get into their good books (which wasn't easy)
you needed to do some pretty horrible things such as killing
your children as a sacrifice.

Now that sort of stuff doesn't sound too good to you and me
(especially if you're a child!) and it *definitely* didn't get God's
seal of approval.
The Canaanites' wicked ways absolutely appalled God.
God had been very patient with the Canaanites over the years
but they had absolutely no intention of stopping what they were
doing.
God had finally decided that enough was enough and now was
the time to call a halt to their vile way of life and the Israelites
were going to be given the job of wiping them off the face of
the earth.

Team Talk

Just before Joshua and the Israelites marched out to conquer Canaan, God had a few things he wanted to say to Joshua...

I'll bet Joshua felt a whole lot better knowing that God was on *his* side.

To get to Canaan the Israelites needed to cross the Jordan river. They camped nearby for three days while they waited for the green light from God to go.

Then the instructions came...

The priests are to go out in front of you carrying the Ark of the covenant...keep a distance of 1,000 yards between you and the Ark...tell the priests to go up to the water's edge...tell them to set foot in the Jordan...its waters will be cut off downstream and stand up in a heap....

Boring Bible Fact: The Ark of the Covenant was a special box that contained the evidence of some of God's amazing miracles he'd done for the Israelites in the past. It was so special that if you touched it without God's permission you'd die. No wonder the Israelites had to keep their distance!

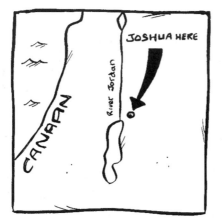

When Joshua and the Israelites arrived at the Jordan it was in full flood but as soon as the priests dipped their feet into it the water stopped flowing, just like God had promised.

While the priests stood in the middle of the dry river bed, the Israelites crossed over to the other side.

As soon as the priests had crossed, and were safely over, the waters flowed back.

Not only did this amazing miracle remind the Israelites how powerful God was but it also sent fear into the hearts of the Canaanites when word reached their ears of what had happened.

Battle Stations!

With their feet firmly set in Canaan, the Israelites were now ready to begin conquering the land.

With so many of the Canaanites living in walled cities, it was going to be a long job.

Joshua planned to start his conquering round about the middle of Canaan and then

gradually move out from there, taking one city at a time. And the first city on Joshua's hit list was **Jericho**.

God had already appeared to Joshua to tell him that the city was his for the taking but how, exactly, were they expected to invade a city without battering rams or any equipment for shattering those massive, thick stone walls?

While Joshua tried to rack his brains for a good idea God came to the rescue with his own battle plan...

MARCH ROUND THE CITY ONCE WITH ALL THE ARMED MEN. DO THIS FOR SIX DAYS. MAKE SEVEN PRIESTS CARRY TRUMPETS OR RAMS' HORNS IN FRONT OF THE ARK. ON THE SEVENTH DAY, MARCH AROUND THE CITY SEVEN TIMES, WITH THE PRIESTS BLOWING THE TRUMPETS. WHEN YOU HEAR THEM SOUND A LONG BLAST ON THE TRUMPETS, MAKE ALL THE PEOPLE GIVE A SHOUT, THEN THE WALL OF THE CITY WILL COLLAPSE AND THE PEOPLE WILL GO UP, EVERY MAN, STRAIGHT IN!

Joshua knew better than to question God.

He simply got the Israelites ready and advanced on Jericho.

For six days, once a day, the Israelites marched around the city, just like God had told them to and then they returned to their camp.

Day Seven

At last the day had arrived.

I wonder what was going through everyone's mind.

Did the Israelites seriously expect to conquer Jericho doing it God's way?

Were the people of Jericho having a good old laugh at the Israelites' weird daily walk round the block?

Well, whatever anyone thought or felt, time was up.

With the priests up front, the Israelites began their seven circuits of Jericho.

Round they went once, round they went twice, three times, four times, fives times, six times and then, with a blast from their trumpets, the Bible tells us that the priests set off around Jericho one last time.

Then Joshua gave the order...

Without the Israelites even lifting a finger the walls of Jericho collapsed into a heap.
Joshua and this army charged in and destroyed every living thing in that wicked city and burnt it to the ground.

The Israelites' conquest of Canaan had begun and with God on their side they had their first victory firmly under their belt.
Before the Israelites moved on to conquer their next city, Joshua pronounced a curse on Jericho which went something like this...

Fascinating Fact:

400 years later, a guy called Hiel from Bethel tried to rebuild Jericho. When he laid the foundation, his eldest son, Abiram, died and when he built the gates, his youngest son, Segub, died. Just like Joshua said they would.

Even with God on their side, it took the Israelites many years to conquer Canaan and even then there were bits of it that they never quite succeeded in taking.

That often made life very difficult for the Israelites and it also meant that some of the Canaanites, wicked ways spoiled things between them and God.

Now, you're probably wondering at this point why this book is called *Catastrophic Kings* when we've not even mentioned one single king yet?

Well, hold your horses for a bit longer, we'll be getting to them, don't you worry, but first, how about one or two more stories from the Israelites first few years in what the Bible calls 'The Promised Land'.

Canaan Conquest No. 1 - The Battle Of Ai

The Israelites marched a few miles to the west of Jericho to a place called AI which looked to them like an easy peasy target.

Unfortunately for the Israelites, they were about to suffer their first defeat and it was all down to one man called Aachan.

Aachan had disobeyed God by keeping for himself some of the booty plundered from their raid on Jericho rather than handing it over to leaders of Israel.

The Israelites had 36 of their men killed when they first tried to attack AI and when Joshua discovered that Aachan's wrongdoing had caused God to withdraw his help from Israel, Aachan and his entire family were executed.

With the problem of Aachan sorted, the Israelites were back on track and God promised them that...

I HAVE DELIVERED THE KING OF AI INTO YOUR HANDS.

That's better!

Joshua chose 30,000 of his best fighting men and got ready to attack.

Have a look at Joshua's clever strategy...

ATTACK ON AI

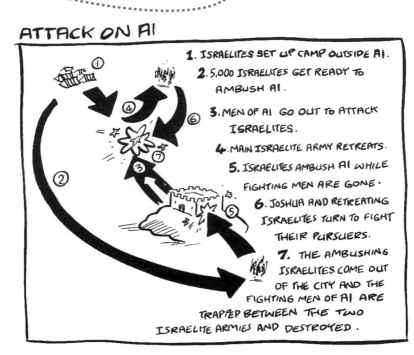

1. ISRAELITES SET UP CAMP OUTSIDE AI.
2. 5,000 ISRAELITES GET READY TO AMBUSH AI.
3. MEN OF AI GO OUT TO ATTACK ISRAELITES.
4. MAIN ISRAELITE ARMY RETREATS.
5. ISRAELITES AMBUSH AI WHILE FIGHTING MEN ARE GONE.
6. JOSHUA AND RETREATING ISRAELITES TURN TO FIGHT THEIR PURSUERS.
7. THE AMBUSHING ISRAELITES COME OUT OF THE CITY AND THE FIGHTING MEN OF AI ARE TRAPPED BETWEEN THE TWO ISRAELITE ARMIES AND DESTROYED.

With God on their side, the Israelites were invincible!

Canaan Conquest No. 2 - The Battle Of The Kings

Aachan wasn't the *only* one to do something silly. When the Gibeonites, some near neighbours of the Israelites, found out that they were on the Israelites' hit list they tricked the Israelites into making a treaty with them so they wouldn't be harmed.

MY HIT LIST

~~JERICHO~~
~~AI~~
GIBEON

Instead they ended up serving the Israelites cutting wood and carrying water which I suppose is a lot better than having your head chopped off.

Meanwhile, a whole bunch of kings from all over Canaan decided to get their own back on the Gibeonites for selling out to the Israelites.

They surrounded Gibeon and got ready to attack it.

The Gibeonites decided there was only one course of action left open to them...

Joshua and the entire Israelite army marched all night and took the Gibeonites' attackers by surprise.

God threw them into complete confusion as Israel advanced against them.

Even as they fled there was no escape and the Bible says that God hurled huge hailstones onto them killing more of them than the Israelites had done with their swords.

It was a long battle and Joshua wanted to make certain that all of the enemy was destroyed so he did something rather unusual...

The Bible tells us that at Joshua's command, the sun stood still in the middle of the sky and did not go down for a whole day until Joshua and the Israelite army had completely conquered their enemies.

They didn't want them escaping back into the safety of their walled cities. That would drag the battle out over days if not weeks. It was now or never.

Fascinating Fact:

Scientists and astronomers have discovered that almost 24 hours have been inserted into history for which there is no explanation. There are also accounts from the records of other ancient nations such as Egypt, India, China, and Aboriginal and Native American peoples that speak of an extra long day occurring.

Joshua lived to the good old age of 110 but before he died he divided up the land between all of the tribes of Israel.

He wasn't giving it to them to keep, it was just on loan from God.
And they couldn't divide it up into smaller bits or sell it because it wasn't theirs to sell.
As I mentioned earlier, the Israelites still had their work cut out trying to get rid of the Canaanites but more of that later.

DIVISION OF THE LAND

ASHER
NAPHTALI
ZEBULUN
ISSACHAR
MANASSEH
EPHRAIM   GAD
BENJAMIN
DAN
JUDAH   REUBEN
SIMEON

Before Joshua popped his clogs it was time to give the Israelites one last pep talk.

Joshua's Top Ten Tips To The Israelites

1 Obey God's laws.
2 Don't neglect any part of the law.
3 Don't associate with the other nations living among you.
4 Don't speak the names of their gods.
5 Don't use those names in vows.
6 Don't bow down to those gods.
7 Love the Lord your God.
8 Don't marry someone from another nation.
9 Be loyal to God.
10 Honour God and serve him faithfully.

With that, Joshua breathed his last and was buried in the hill-country of Ephraim.

Hey, hang on a minute, Joshua, don't die yet, you haven't chosen a new leader for Israel to take your place...

Oops!

Too late.

On second thoughts, God probably didn't want them to have any more human leaders anyway.

Now that they were settled in Canaan, each in their own tribes, I reckon God expected everyone to look to *him* for guidance and protection.

Unfortunately, this was wishful thinking.

The next 200 years or so of Israel's history looked a bit like this.

As that whole generation of people who had seen God's mighty miracles died, so the next generation of Israelites growing up began to turn away from God.

Here's how the Bible puts it...

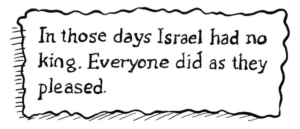

In those days Israel had no king. Everyone did as they pleased.

This was not good news.

If the Israelites were going to completely conquer every last inch of Canaan then they needed God's help.

We've already seen what happened when he **wasn't** with them, with the story of silly Aachan.

When the Israelites realised that things were going from bad to worse they decided that there was only one thing left for them to do...

Hmm, I wonder what God will do?
I know what most of us would say...

Fortunately for the Israelites God isn't like that.

Here's a list of some of the things that the Bible says that God **is like...**

That sort of changes things doesn't it?

Here's what God did every time the Israelites cried out to him for help.

He sent them a leader, which the Bible calls a '**judge**'.

They weren't like this sort of judge...

more like this...

For the next couple of hundred years the Israelites' realtionship with God was a bit like a yo-yo.

One minute it was up, the next it was down.

One minute they were trying to live lives that pleased God, then the next they were doing their own thing again.

As we've already discovered, when they trusted in God, things went well but when they went their own way then things went wrong.

Because God was patient and forgiving (like we've seen in the list), whenever they said "sorry" to God for being disobedient he sent them a *new* leader to help them out of the mess they'd got themselves into.

All in all, the Israelites got through twelve judges, that's one for each tribe of Israel.

Before we finally get to the *Catastophic Kings* we've all been waiting for, let's whizz through a few of the judges and take a peek at what sort of people they were.

You might well have heard of at least one of them.

His name was Samson but first let's check out Ehud

THE JUDGES INVESTIGATED!

NAME: Ehud

BACKGROUND: From the tribe of Benjamin.

PECULIARITIES: He was left-handed.

GREATEST ACHIEVEMENT: Assassinated King Eglon of Moab who was giving the Israelites a mega hard time. Ehud went up to Eglon with gifts from the Israelites. He also hid a whopping great sword on the **opposite** side to where people usually kept theirs (so it wouldn't be discovered), because he was left-handed, and then, when he was alone with the king, he plunged the sword into his belly.

Eglon was a bit of a porker and the Bible says that sword went in so deep that even its handle was swallowed up by the king's fat stomach! Ugh!

ER, CAN I HAVE MY SWORD BACK, PLEASE ?

That day the Israelites defeated the Moabites and there was peace in the land for 80 years.

NAME: Deborah

BACKGROUND: Wife of Lappidoth. Lived in Ephraim.

PECULIARITIES: Used to sit under a palm tree to do her 'judging'.

GREATEST ACHIEVEMENT: Headed up the Israelite army to attack the army of King Jabin of Hazor. The 10,000 Israelites slaughtered Jabin's army and his 900 charioteers. His commander, Sisera, scarpered and took refuge in a nomad's tent. He was so flaked out that he dropped off to sleep and was promptly killed by a lady called Jael whose tent it was. If you really want to know the gory details, she killed him by hammering a tent peg into his head. Bet **that's** put you off camping for life hasn't it?

(The Bible tells us that there was then peace in the land for 40 years)

THE JUDGES INVESTIGATED!

NAME: Gideon

BACKGROUND: From the tribe of Manasseh. Lived in a village called Ophrah (nothing to do with a well-known TV presenter!)

PECULIARITIES: Gideon got God to prove that he was on his side by using a sheep's fleece. If it remained dry while the ground was wet with morning dew then that would be his sign. It was. In fact, Gideon actually asked God for **three** signs in total, and God convinced Gideon 100%.

GREATEST ACHIEVEMENT: With God's help, some trumpets, some torches, some swords and just 300 men, Gideon defeated the entire Midianite army.

(The Bible says that there was peace in the land for 40 years, until Gideon died.)

And last, but not least, the man you've all been waiting for...Samson!

THE JUDGES INVESTIGATED!

NAME: *Samson*
BACKGROUND: *From the tribe of Dan. Lived in a town called Zorah.*
PECULIARITIES: *Samson's mum had dedicated him to God from birth. Because of that he wouldn't be allowed to drink wine or beer or have his hair cut.*
GREATEST ACHIEVEMENT: *During Samson's lifetime it was the Philistines who were giving the Israelites a hard time. Samson had a reputation for being incredibly strong which was all down to God being with him.*
*(He'd once even killed a lion **bare**-handed - I wonder how he killed bears?)*

The Philistines knew that if they could get rid of Samson then the Israelites would be an even easier target. Samson had a bit of a weakness for women and he fell in love with Delilah, a Philistine. If you remember, God had told the Israelites that on no account must they marry a foreigner because they worshipped other gods.

After much persuasion, Delilah managed to discover the secret of Samson's strength. While he was aleep, Samson's hair was cut, and his strength was gone. He was captured, had his eyes gouged out (ouch!) and he was then chucked into prison.

In time, his hair grew back and with it his strength.

When all the Philistine kings were gathered together in the temple of their god, Dagon, to offer sacrifices, Samson was called upon to entertain them.

With the temple packed with thousands of Philistines, Samson stood between the supporting pillars of the temple and asked God for the strength to do one last thing.

Samson pushed the pillars with all his might and the temple crashed to the ground killing everyone inside it.

So that was that.

Throughout the whole time that Israel was ruled by judges nothing really changed much. They only got through it all by the skin of their teeth and obviously God's goodness.

In the main, that was really the end of the judges as we know it.

Boring Bible Fact: The Bible says that after everything that God had done for them during the time of the judges the Israelites *still* did exactly as they pleased.

Anyway, now for the moment you've all been waiting for.
It's time for those *Catastrophic Kings*.
Just one small problem.
We can't quite get to them without some sort of link.

What we need is some sort of bridge to get us there.

Hmm, not *quite* what I had in mind.
How about something like this?....

That's more like it!
Yes, I know it's a person not a bridge.
Now, off you go and find out about the *Catastrophic Kings*.

What do you mean you haven't got a clue what I'm talking about?

Don't you know who Samuel is?

Oh dear, that's a pity because it's really important.

I suppose there's nothing for it, we're just going to have to play the world's least popular board game to get us to those elusive *Catastrophic Kings*.

Turn the page and let's all have a game of good old...

'GET-TO-THOSE-

(Catchy name, huh!)

START

1

2 HANNAH ASKS GOD FOR A CHILD

3

4 MISS A GO

5

6 SAMUEL IS BORN

7

8 GO BACK ONE PLACE

9

10 HANNAH GIVES SAMUEL BACK TO GOD

11

12

13 SAMUEL IS BROUGHT UP IN THE TABERNACLE

14

15

16 THROW DICE AGAIN

17

18 GOD WAKES SAMUEL THREE TIMES TO SPEAK TO HIM

KINGS'

31 GOD GIVES THEM WHAT THEY WANT AND SAMUEL SETS OUT TO FIND A **KING...**

32 FINISH

19

20

30

21 SAMUEL GROWS UP TO BE THE GO-BETWEEN FOR GOD AND THE ISRAELITES

29 ISRAELITES WON'T LISTEN

28

22

27 SAMUEL WARNS THEM THAT A KING IS NOT A GOOD IDEA

23 ISRAEL DEMANDS TO HAVE A KING LIKE THE OTHER NATIONS

26 GO FORWARD A SPACE

24

25

So, Samuel was the man God used to take the Israelites *from* the time of the judges *to* the time of the kings.

But by asking for a king, the Israelites had, in effect, rejected *God* as their king.

And this is how God had warned the Israelites that a *human* king would treat them...

HE WILL MAKE SOLDIERS OF YOUR SONS, THEY WILL HAVE TO PLOUGH HIS FIELDS AND HARVEST HIS CROPS. YOUR DAUGHTERS WILL WORK AS HIS COOKS AND BAKERS, HE WILL TAKE YOUR BEST FIELDS, VINEYARDS AND OLIVE GROVES, HE WILL TAKE A TENTH OF YOUR CORN AND YOUR GRAPES. HE WILL TAKE YOUR SERVANTS AND YOUR BEST CATTLE AND YOU YOURSELVES WILL BECOME SLAVES.

After hearing all that you'd think that the Israelites would change their minds, but no.
This was their reply...
They're determined, I'll give them that!

So, here begins the stories of three of Israel's greatest kings. As a special treat we've given each of them their own little book for being so patient with us.
Why have we called them *Catastrophic Kings* you ask?
Well, you're soon to find out that even the *best* of God's leaders can foul up big time.

Catastrophic Kings
BOOK ONE
THE RISE
AND FALL
OF
COOL SAUL

Chapter One – Israel's First Ever King

When it came to choosing a king it wasn't up to the Israelites and it wasn't even up to Samuel. It was *God* who did the choosing and *he* already knew *exactly* who he wanted for the job.

His name was Saul and the Bible says he came from quite a well-to-do family.

Saul was handsome, he was tall and he was young.

One day, some of his dad's donkeys went astray (or should I say ASS-tray?), so Saul and one of the servants went off in hot pursuit.

They hunted high and low but they were nowhere to be found. They'd been gone some time and Saul figured that his dad would soon stop worrying about the donkeys and start fretting about him instead.

The holy man that they were talking about was none other than Samuel.

Saul and his servant eventually tracked Samuel down as he was on his way to worship God.

Saul turning up was no big surprise to Samuel, in fact God had told him about Saul the day before so Samuel was expecting him.

I'll bet the pair of them were gobsmacked by what Samuel said. The very next morning, as Samuel sent them on their way, he told Saul to let his servant go on ahead.

Then, taking a jar of olive oil, he poured it over Saul's head and said...

THE LORD GOD ANOINTS YOU AS RULER OF HIS PEOPLE, ISRAEL. YOU WILL RULE HIS PEOPLE AND PROTECT THEM FROM THEIR ENEMIES.

Boring Bible Fact: Anointing with oil was God's way of marking out people who he was going to use in a special way.

Chapter Two - Saul Is Declared King

It wasn't much use making someone king if nobody knew about it.

Samuel gathered together the Israelite nation at a place called Mizpah and reminded them of all the good things God had done for them in the past and once again warned them what a bad move having a human king was.

With all that out of the way the time had come to tell the Israelites who was going to be their first king.

If you've ever seen an awards ceremony on TV you'll notice how they always seem to keep you in suspense until the very last moment.

It was the same with Samuel.
First he made each of Israel's twelve tribes come forward.

Then Samuel made the tribe of Benjamin come forward, family by family.

And finally, Samuel made the family of Matri come forward.

Whoops! Looks like there's a slight technical hitch.
They can't find Saul.
And no wonder.
Stage fright must have got the better of him because he was
hiding behind the supplies.
Saul was reluctantly dragged out and proclaimed king.

Chapter Three - Saul's First Victory

Only one month after becoming king, Saul had his first big chance to prove himself.

The Ammonites were beseiging Jabesh, one of the Israelites' towns.

King Nabash of Ammon was threatening to gouge out one of everyone's eyes even if they made a treaty. (They had a thing about gouging out eyes in those days, didn't they?)

Things weren't looking good but they managed to get word to Saul of their plight.

The Bible says that the Spirit of God took control of Saul and he became furious.
He cut up two oxen into pieces and had them sent throughout Israel with a rather disturbing warning...

To be honest, the Israelites were beginnning to get the hang of this business about obeying God and were so frightened of what God might do to them if they *didn't* do what Saul said, they turned up for battle, every last man.

330,000 fighting men mounted a surprise early morning attack on the Ammonites and slaughtered them.

What a victory for the Israelites!

What a boost for Saul as their new king!

Boring Bible Fact: Samuel wanted to keep the Israelites on their toes and remind them one more time what a terrible decision they had made asking for a king. To put the fear of God into them he asked God to send thunder and rain in the middle of the dry season. It did the trick. It scared the pants off them and they begged God not to kill them.

Chapter Four - Saul's Big BooBoo

Saul and his troops were off to make war with the Philistines. Saul's son, Jonathan, scored a bullseye and killed the Philistine's commander which *really* riled them.

They brought out the biggest army they could muster with 30,000 war chariots, 6,000 horsemen and a massive army of foot soldiers.

The Israelites were no match for the Philistines and retreated into the rocks and caves of the hillside.

The situation was desperate and Samuel had been called for.

He'd promised to be there in seven days.

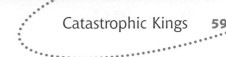

As day seven arrived, the scared Israelites began to desert Saul in their droves.

Saul didn't know what to do.

Then he had an idea...

If you've read any of the earlier Boring Bible books you'll have learned all about how the Israelites made different sorts of sacrifices on stone altars to please God.

They only did this because God had told them to do it.

God had given the job of burning the sacrifices to priests taken from one of the Israelite tribes.

It wasn't something *anyone* could do willy nilly.

It was a serious business and woe betide anyone who disobeyed God in this matter.

It was still the seventh day when Samuel turned up on the scene, just like he'd promised he would.
Saul's impatience was going to cost him dear.

YOU'VE DONE A FOOLISH THING SAUL! YOU HAVE DISOBEYED GOD AND NOW YOUR RULE WILL COME TO AN END. GOD WILL FIND ANOTHER KING FOR ISRAEL!

In fact, it was some time before Saul was actually replaced as king and although God gave him success in some of his battles Saul's actions only seemed to go from bad to worse from then on.

A Couple Of Saul's Bad Moves

1 Once when the Israelites were fighting the Philistines, Saul made a crazy oath that any of them who ate food before they had beaten their enemy would be put to death.
Saul's son, Jonathan, who knew nothing of his father's curse, dipped a stick he was carrying into a honeycomb and ate the honey. When Saul found out, he was all for carrying out his death threat but the rest of the Israelites stood by Jonathan and persuaded Saul to change his mind.
I'll bet that'll make you think twice about tucking into your tea before your parents tell you!

2 Another time, God told Saul to take the Israelites to attack and destroy the Amalekites and everything they had because they were Israel's enemies from of old. For fear of upsetting his men,

Saul allowed them to keep some of the Amalekites' animals.
Not only that but Saul had spared the life of Agag, the
Amalekite king.
Once again, Saul had disobeyed God.
Samuel took it upon himself to finish the job.
He had king Agag brought before him in fear and trembling...

At which Samuel cut King Agag to pieces.
Messy but necessary.

Samuel and Saul went their separate ways and they never saw
each other ever again.

The Bible tells us that God was sorry that he had ever made Saul king.

At this point of the story we've got a bit of a problem.
You're about to be introduced to our next *Catastrophic King* but *his* story does quite a bit of overlapping with Saul's story.
What we'll do is maybe get our next king started then see how things go.
How does that sound?
Just before you meet him, God's got a few things he wants to say to Samuel.

Well, no arguing with that then.
Which leads us rather nicely into our next *Catastrophic King*...

Catastrophic Kings

BOOK TWO

THE DARING, DAZZLING AND DASTARDLY DAYS OF INDOMITABLE DAVID

Chapter One - Saul's Replacement

Samuel left his home in Ramah and travelled down to Bethlehem to find Israel's next king.

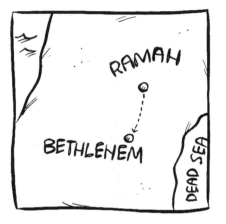

Having Samuel or any man of God come to your town was even more awesome than a president or pop star turning up.

The Bible says that the city leaders of Bethlehem came out to meet Samuel trembling.

They weren't sure whether he'd come with good news or if they'd done something to displease God.

I'll bet they were relieved when Samuel told them why he was there.

With Jesse's sons all lined up before them, Samuel began the task of picking Israel's next king.

But God said...

Next please!

One by one Samuel worked his way through each of Jesse's seven sons.

Perhaps Samuel's gone and made a mistake.

Maybe he heard wrong.

But no, he'd heard right.

It was definitely one of *Jesse's* sons he was looking for.

Jesse immediately sent for his youngest son while everyone waited with bated breath to see what Samuel would do. David was a handsome and healthy young man and the Bible says that his eyes sparkled...

God said to Samuel...

As David the shepherd boy was anointed king of Israel two things happened.
Firstly, David was filled with God's Spirit.
And secondly, God's Spirit left Saul.
But as far as Saul was concerned things went even *more* downhill.
Because of his disobedience to God an evil spirit came upon him instead and tormented him something rotten.

Strange But True!

All through the Bible there are lots of weird coincidences and one of them happened between none other than Saul and David.

Saul's servants suggested that he employ a musician to soothe away the tormenting evil spirit.

And guess who the Bible tells us was nifty on the harp?

Yep, it was David!

Would you believe it, but David ended up working for Saul as his harpist.

Obviously nobody had told him that David had been picked as his replacement as king, which is probably just as well.

Who knows what Saul would have done if he'd known?

The good news was that David did such a good job of his 'harping' that Saul even let him carry his weapons for him.

Chapter Two - David's Big, Big Problem

Even if you don't know much else about David you'll probably have heard about his first victory in battle.

But just in case you want to hear it again, here's the story of...

David And Goliath

Israel's favourite enemy, the Philistines, had gathered to do battle here...

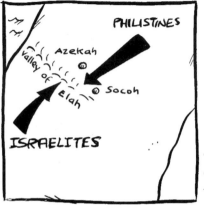

...and with the Philistines on one hill, the Israelites on the other and a valley between them you could cut the atmosphere with a knife.

The Israelites and the Philistines were fairly well matched except for one thing.
The Philistines had a secret weapon.
Introducing....

GOLIATH

IRON POINT WEIGHS 7 Kilogrammes (15 Pounds)

BRONZE HELMET

NASTY FROWN

COAT OF ARMOUR WEIGHING 57 Kilogrammes (125 Pounds)

3 METRES (9 FEET)

BRONZE JAVELIN

LONG GREAVES

HANDLE WITH CARE!

UNFASHIONABLE FOOTWEAR

With his shield-bearer out in front, he came out every day, for 40 days, and taunted the poor old Israelites.

COME OUT AND FIGHT! CHOOSE A MAN AND IF **HE** KILLS ME, THE PHILISTINES WILL BE YOUR SUBJECTS AND IF **I** WIN, THEN YOU WILL SERVE US!

The Israelites were scared silly. Goliath was ginormous.
Any man who went out to fight him, hand to hand, wouldn't stand a chance.
One day, David turned up on the scene to bring his three eldest brothers, who were in Saul's army, a packed lunch.
David couldn't believe that Saul and his men would let a Philistine threaten God's army in such a way.
David managed to persuade Saul to let him have a go at fighting Goliath.

I'VE BEEN KEEPING MY FATHER'S SHEEP! I'VE KILLED LIONS **AND** BEARS PROTECTING THE SHEEP! THE GOD WHO HELPED ME DO **THAT** WILL ALSO HELP ME DEFEAT THIS PHILISTINE!

Saul couldn't argue with that and to be honest there was hardly a long line of volunteers queuing to take on Goliath.

Just for good measure, David cut off Goliath's head but I was too squeamish to draw *that* bit of the story.

When the Philistines realised their champion fighter was dead they ran for it.

The Israelites followed in hot pursuit and killed them.

David was a hero but Saul was jealous of him.

It didn't help that Saul's son Jonathan and David became best friends.

Then, to rub salt into the wound, when the Israelites came back from beating the Philistines the Israelite women burst into song...

Chapter Three - David Has To Watch His Back

Saul didn't like David getting more of the credit than him.

Saul did everything he could to get his own back but nothing seemed to work.

Saul's Ridiculous Revenges

- Saul tried to marry David off to his daughter Michal, who was a bit of hard work.
- Saul tried to spear him with his javelin.
- Saul sent him into battle with the hope that the Philistines would kill him.

All without success!

David realised that Saul was bent on killing him and escaped to the countryside and hid in a cave.

Saul would not give up.

He took 600 fighting men and searched high and low for David, killing anyone and everyone who he felt was shielding David.

What happened next was really odd.

Now, let's be honest, there are some things you would **not** expect to find in the Bible but the Bible never minces words. When you read a story in the Bible it tells it just as it happened, warts and all. (That means even the grotty bits are left in.)

While David and his men were hiding in one of these caves, who should come in but Saul.

And you'll never guess in a million years why he'd slipped away from his troops for five minutes...or would you?

Go on have a guess!

I think Saul had slipped into the cave because...

_____

Well, the answer you're looking for, and you might well have guessed it, is that he was going in there to 'relieve himself' or at least that's how the Bible puts it, you probably say something different but we all know what we mean, don't we?

David could have killed Saul where he stood, that's what his fellow fighting men wanted him to do.

But David couldn't bring himself to murder someone that God had anointed king even though he was out to get David.

All David did was to quietly snip off a corner of Saul's robe but even *that* made David feel so guilty.

When Saul had left, David went outside and fell face down on the ground and let Saul know what he had just done.

When Saul realised that David had spared his life he agreed not to pursue him any more.

In time both Samuel and Saul died but Saul ended up taking his own life after a terrible defeat which killed his three sons.

Chapter Four - King At Last

When David was 30 years old he was officially made king.

All those years of training as a shepherd caring for the sheep and as a soldier fighting for the people were at last put to good use.

David would be a strong and powerful king but he would also be a king who cared.

That's just the way God wanted it.

Of all the kings of Israel mentioned in the Bible, King David is the most important.

The Bible says that his success was down to one thing.

He was a man after God's own heart.

That means he was concerned about the same things as God.

Boring Bible Fact: King David, as well as being a pretty mean harpist also wrote songs. The Bible calls them Psalms,(but you don't sound the 'p') and there's 150 of them in all.

David was the best known Psalmist (that's what someone who writes Psalms is called) because he wrote so many of them.

The Psalms were about anything and everything. Sometimes they started off by telling God how hard life was but ended up praising God for his goodness.

Other times they're reminders of what God is like and the things he's done.

Just like songs, the Psalms are also made up of verses. The longest Psalm (number 119) has 176 verses and the shortest one (number 117) has just two!

Here's our pick of the Psalm charts...

At number 3, that noisy favourite...Psalm 150.

Praise the Lord!
Praise God in His Temple!
Praise his strength in heaven!
Praise him for the mighty things he has done.
Praise his supreme greatness.

Praise him with trumpets.
Praise him with harps and lyres.
Praise him with drums and dancing.
Praise him with harps and flutes.
Praise him with cymbals.
Praise him with loud cymbals.
Praise the Lord, all living creatures!
Praise the Lord!

At number 2, we have a new entry...Psalm 100.

Sing to the Lord, all the world!
Worship the Lord with joy;
come before him with happy songs!

Acknowledge that the Lord is God.
He made us and we belong to him;
we are his people, we are his flock.

Enter the temple gates with thanksgiving,
go into into its courts with praise.
Give thanks to him him and praise him.
The Lord is good;
his love is eternal
and his faithfulness lasts for ever.

**And still at number 1 for another week is ...Psalm 23.
Take it away...**

The Lord is my shepherd;
I have everything I need.
He lets me rest in fields of green grass
and leads me to quiet pools of fresh water.
He gives me strength.
He guides me in the right paths,
as he has promised.
Even if I go through the deepest darkness,
I will not be afraid, Lord,
for you are with me.
Your shepherd`s rod and staff protect me.

Chapter Five – Naughty but Nice

All in all, David ruled as king for 40 years.
In that time David did some spectacularly good things but he also did some spectacularly bad things.

One Of The Good Things That King David Did

One of the good things that David did when he became king was to bring the Ark of the Covenant up from Baalah, in Judah, to Israel's main city, Jerusalem.
This special box held a place of honour among the Israelites as it represented God's presence and protection with them. The Ark (or box as it was sometimes called), was put onto a cart with oxen to pull it.

The Israelites danced and sang as they led the happy procession back to Jerusalem.
Disaster struck along the way when the oxen stumbled and one of the men looking after the Ark reached out to grab it.
God killed the man stone dead where he stood for not showing him respect.
That **really** put the fear of God into everyone.
David turned off the road and left the Ark at the home of a man called Obed Edom while he went back home to work out what on earth to do with it.

All the while it was there Obed Edom and his family got blessed by God.

...thought David and promptly went back to fetch the Ark and finish the job of bringing it back to Jerusalem.

It was a great day of celebration in Israel and David danced and shouted at the front of the procession wearing only a linen skirt!

At long last the Ark was back where it belonged in the tabernacle tent where the Israelites offered their sacrifices to God.

One Of The Bad Things That King David Did

What do you think of when you think of spring? Bunnies, daffodils, spring-cleaning?

Well, if you were in King David's boots it would be something more like fighting, killing and doing battle.

The Bible says that at spring, when kings usually go to war, King David stayed at home.

The Israelite army, led by his commander Joab, *still* went out to fight, but not David.

The Bible doesn't say why but maybe he just wanted a year off, who knows?

One day, after having an afternoon snooze, he took a stroll round the palace roof and clapped eyes on a beautiful woman having a bath.

He found out her name was Bathsheba and she was the wife of Uriah the Hittite, one of his soldiers.

Bathsheba was brought to King David who then slept with her so she became pregnant, which was bad enough in itself.

David then made matters worse by trying to cover up his sin by making sure Uriah got killed in battle.

God doesn't miss a trick and punished David by allowing the baby to die.

Boring Bible Fact: You might be wondering what a 'sin' is. Sin is when you do something that God says you *shouldn't* do or when you don't do something God says you *should* do!

Another One Of The Good Things That King David Did

One time, when King David was in a particularly good mood, he decided that he wanted to show kindness to any of King Saul's family who might still be alive. This wasn't because he had suddenly forgotten what a nasty piece of work Saul had been. It was because he had fond memories of Saul's son, Jonathan. They'd been best friends and he wanted to do something in memory of Jonathan.

David discovered that one of Jonathan's own sons,

Mephibosheth (try saying *that* quickly), who was crippled in both feet, was still living.

For one moment Mephibosheth thought King David was about to take revenge for the way his grandfather, Saul, had treated David.

But no. Instead, David gave back to Mephibosheth everything that belonged to Saul's family including all their land.

And to cap it all David announced that...

MEPHIBOSHETH WILL ALWAYS BE A GUEST AT MY TABLE!

In fact, Mephibosheth became almost like one of David's own sons.

What a nice man King David was.

King David's life was sometimes up and sometimes down but he never forgot the God of Israel who had made him king.

When push came to shove, it was pleasing God that made David tick.

David was to become Israel's most famous king and he even had a Christmas carol written about him.

Before David died, he made Solomon, his son by Bathsheba, Israel's next king. Solomon wasn't next in line to the throne but David knew that Solomon would be a man who put God first so he made certain that Solomon was crowned king *despite* what other people thought best.

The good news is that Solomon was going to be a good king for Israel.

Isn't it amazing that even out of the bad thing that David and Bathsheba did, God was still able to bring out something good. But don't forget, that's what God was doing by creating the Israelite nation in the first place. He had taken out a whole bunch of people from the rotten and spoiled human race and was going to use *them* to patch up his friendship with people.

Catastrophic Kings

BOOK THREE

THE WONDERFULLY WEALTHY WORLD OF WISE SOLOMON

Chapter One – A Wise Decision

Just before King David died he gave his son, Solomon, some really good advice...

Seems like good advice.

One of the first things Solomon did was to marry the king of Egypt's daughter. That way he wouldn't have to worry about being invaded by the Egyptians.

Nice move, Solomon!

Then, one night, Solomon had a dream.

Nothing unusual about that I hear you say.

Thanks.

But Solomon's dream wasn't one of those ones when you're being chased by a giant lettuce and you can't escape or one which you can't remember anything

about when you wake up.

In Solomon's dream, God appeared to him and asked him a question.

> ## WHAT WOULD YOU LIKE ME TO GIVE YOU?

Good question!

Before I tell you what Solomon asked for, what would *you* ask for if God said you could have *anything* you wanted?

a A million pounds.

b A big house.

c To be famous.

d To be made president.

e Anything else.

Here's what Solomon asked God for...

> ## GIVE ME THE **WISDOM** TO RULE YOUR PEOPLE WITH JUSTICE AND TO KNOW THE DIFFERENCE BETWEEN GOOD AND EVIL.

Was wisdom on *your* list?

The Bible says that God was so pleased with Solomon's reply that he said he would not only give him what he'd asked for but he'd also give him wealth, honour and a long life.

Imagine that sort of decision being made by the judges in our law courts.

With wisdom like that people would think twice about bringing untrue claims to court, wouldn't they?

The Bible says that when the rest of Israel heard about Solomon's decision they were all filled with deep respect for him.

Chapter Two - Didn't They Do Well?

Just like God promised, Solomon and the Israelites prospered. Here's some facts the Bible gives us...

• Solomon was at peace with all his neighbours.
• Each family had its own grape vines and fig trees.
• Solomon had 40,000 chariot and cavalry horses.
• Solomon was wiser than all the wise men in the other lands.
• Solomon had amazing knowledge about nature and plants.
• Everyone had everything they needed.
• Silver was as common as stone.
• People came from all over the world to listen to Solomon's wisdom.

Unfinished Business

There'd been one thing that Solomon's dad had been really desperate to do but had not got round to because he'd been so busy fighting the surrounding nations.

King David had his heart set on building a permanent building for making sacrifices to God and for God to live in.

The Temple he had planned was going to replace the portable tabernacle that the Israelites had been carrying around as they travelled from place to place before they finally settled in Canaan, or Israel as they now called it.

Solomon was now going to finish in reality the job his dad had begun on paper.

Chapter Three - Building On His Success

If you're going to build something nowadays, once you've got your plans drafted up, your first port of call is probably going to be the builders' merchant's to pick up all your building materials.

Unfortunately for Solomon, builders' merchants hadn't been invented so he had to get his building materials some other way...

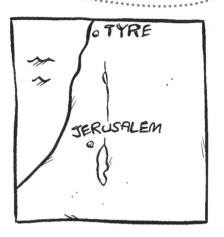

Er, not quite!
Solomon's dad had been best mates with King Hiram of Tyre.
Here's where Tyre is...

One good thing about Tyre was its cedar trees.
The region was positively famous for them.
The cedars of Lebanon (as they were called), were the best timber around so they were just the job for Solomon's magnificent new Temple.
King Hiram was only too happy to help out the son of his old friend.

The plan was that Hiram's skilled woodcutters would chop the trees down, tie them together in rafts and then float them down the coast where Solomon's men would untie them and cart them back to Jerusalem where the Temple was going to be built.
You've probably seen pictures of modern-day logging where they do a similar thing by floating the logs downriver to the sawmill.

It must have been very expensive.
What did all this cost Solomon ?

Cheap at twice the price!

PAY SLIP

JOB:-
Woodcutter

PAY:-
Your daily food

Solomon's Temple Taskforce

30,000 men to work in Lebanon in three groups of 10,000 with one month away and two months back home (wasn't Solomon considerate?).

80,000 men to work in the hillside quarrying stone.

70,000 men to carry the stone.

3,300 men as foremen.

The Temple Plans

One thing that building sites aren't is quiet.

Solomon's Temple was the exception.

The Bible tells us that no noise was made by hammers, axes or any other iron tool while the Temple was being built.

All the noisy stuff was done elsewhere.

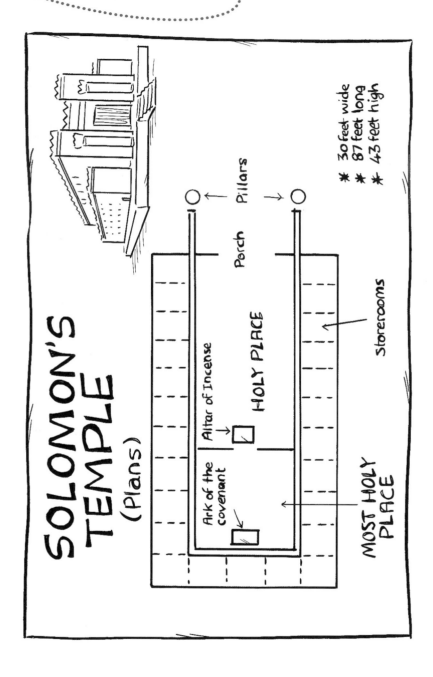

SOLOMON'S TEMPLE
(Plans)

Ark of the covenant

Altar of Incense

HOLY PLACE

MOST HOLY PLACE

Porch   Pillars

Storerooms

* 30 feet wide
* 87 feet long
* 43 feet high

Solomon wasn't just content to build a Temple.
While he was at it, he had a palace built as well.
Together, they took twenty years to complete (seven years for
the Temple and thirteen for the palace) and what a spectacular
sight they must have made.
This had been the biggest building project the Israelites had ever
seen the like of.

It's quite normal for a big building to have an opening
ceremony where someone makes a bit of a speech and then cuts
a ribbon and declares the building open.

After seven long years building the thing, Solomon wasn't going to let the moment pass without making a big splash.

He called together the leaders from all the tribes of Israel together with the priests and the Levites.

With great ceremony, the Ark of the Covenant was brought triumphantly into the Temple.

As the priests were leaving the place was suddenly filled with a cloud shining with dazzling light. It was God himself. It was so awesome they couldn't carry on with their work.

God had come to live in the Temple and to be among his people, the Israelites.

Solomon was totally overwhelmed by the whole thing.

Solomon stood before the people and gave them his address...

No, not that sort of address.
A *speech* sort of address!

I reckon the priests must have been on overtime pay.
The Bible says that Solomon and the Israelites sacrificed 22,000 cattle and 120,000 sheep to God!

The celebrations continued for another seven days and on the eighth day Solomon sent all the people home.

Chapter Four - Wise, Wise, Wise

Some Of Solomon's Other Great Achievements

1   Rebuilt the cities of Hazor, Lower Beth Horon, Baalath, Tamar, Megiddo and Gezer (which Solomon gave as a wedding present to his daughter. Beats getting a toaster!).
2   Made slaves of the Amorites, Hittites, Perizzites, Hivites, Jebusites and the Websites (I made that last one up just in case you were wondering!).
3   He built a fleet of ships.
4   Solomon was also famous for his proverbs (which is just another word for 'wise sayings').

All in all Solomon came up with around 3000 of them, many of which appear in the Bible in a book called none other than...*PROVERBS*.
How original!
Have a look at a few...

Pick Of The Proverbs

People with quick tempers cause a lot of quarrelling and trouble.

The lazy man turns over in bed. He gets no further than a door swinging on its hinges.

If you let a fool deliver a message you might as well cut off your own feet; you are asking for trouble.

Pay close attention to your teacher and learn all you can.

Gossip is so tasty - how we love to swallow it.

If you pay attention when corrected, you are wise.

Stupid people always think they are right. Wise people listen to advice.

Trust in the Lord with all your heart. Never rely on your own understanding.

A nagging wife is like water going drip-drip-drip on a rainy day. How can you keep her quiet?

If you read on a bit further you'll find out why Solomon was the person most experienced to answer that last proverb!

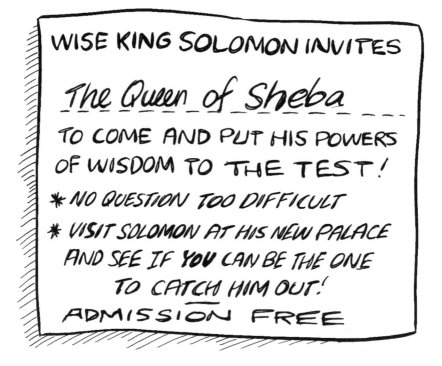

WISE KING SOLOMON INVITES

The Queen of Sheba _ _ _

TO COME AND PUT HIS POWERS OF WISDOM TO THE TEST!

* NO QUESTION TOO DIFFICULT

* VISIT SOLOMON AT HIS NEW PALACE AND SEE IF **YOU** CAN BE THE ONE TO CATCH HIM OUT!

ADMISSION FREE

Such was King Solomon's fame that the Queen of Sheba travelled about 1,200 miles, all the way from Arabia, to put his wisdom to the test.

Along with a large group of attendants, she brought camels loaded down with spices, jewels and gold as gifts.

Every question she asked Solomon, he answered.

There wasn't any question too difficult.

The Bible doesn't actually tell us what she asked.

Perhaps it was something like...

or maybe...

or even...

Whatever questions the Queen of Sheba asked Solomon, one thing is for sure.
She was bowled over by him.

Boring Bible Fact: Solomon's wisdom was so unique he even had an expression named after him. When someone is really wise you say that they have 'the wisdom of Solomon'.

Solomon's wealth grew and grew and grew but it wasn't the only thing that did.
So did the number of his wives.

Chapter Five - Wives, Wives, Wives

In those days, people allowed themselves to have as many wives as they could afford (which caused all manner of problems.)
The Bible says that Solomon had a staggering 700 wives and 300 slave wives.
That's an awful lot of wedding anniversaries to remember!

IT'S THEIR **NAMES** I HAVE TROUBLE REMEMBERING!

Solomon's heart began to turn away from God. The wives he took from the foreign nations that God had forbidden the Israelites to marry brought with them all their foreign gods and it wasn't long before Solomon had started to worship what the Bible calls their 'disgusting gods' like Astarte and Molech. God twice appeared to Solomon to warn him to turn from his sin but Solomon deliberately disobeyed God.

Who knows why King Solomon did such a terrible thing? The Bible doesn't tell us.

As with our two other *Catastrophic Kings*, when they disobeyed God things started to go wrong but in this case it wasn't just Solomon who suffered.

But before all that, it's time to say goodbye to Solomon because his time is up.

Catastrophic Kings

BOOK FOUR

KINGS, KINGS AND EVEN MORE KINGS!

Chapter One - The Parting Of The Ways

You might think that things couldn't get any worse but you're about to find out how wrong you can be!

Over the years to come the Israelites would have 38 more kings (and one queen), but hardly any of them obeyed God or worshipped him.

But before all that, something painful is going to happen to Israel.

Have you ever tried to do the splits where one leg goes one way and the other leg goes the other?

It's painful, isn't it?
I'm afraid I've got some bad news for you...

After Solomon died, his son Rehoboam took over as king. Rehoboam didn't have his dad's wisdom and when the Israelites came complaining to him about all the taxes they had to pay, (that's where a lot of the money to build the Temple came from) he first asked the older men of Israel what he should do...

Hmm, sounds fair to me.
But then Rehoboam consulted his mates for a second opinion and they replied...

Oh, dear.
That's not very nice, is it?
Now what should Rehoboam do?

Put a tick in the box if you think Rehoboam should listen to the old men's advice.

Put a tick in the box if you think Rehoboam should listen to his mates' advice.

Guess what?
Rehoboam listened to his mates.
Sounds like a bad move to me.
I wonder how the Israelites took it?
Well, not surprisingly, the people rebelled.
They weren't going to serve an unfair king.
Which is why Israel split in two.
Two of the tribes decided to stay with Rehoboam and the other ten went their own way.
The ten tribes kept the name 'Israel' while the other two called themselves Judah.

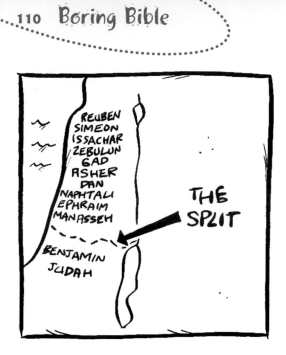

This split was God's punishment for the sin that King David committed with Bathsheba.
Just like God had promised, God's people would from now on be at war with each other.

Let's see what happened to these two kingdoms...

NORTHERN KINGDOM

There was just one small problem for the ten tribes (which still called themselves Israel).

They'd lost Jerusalem *and* the Temple in the split.

That didn't worry Jeroboam, the northern kingdom's first king. He had other ideas...

To stop his people wandering off to the Temple at Jerusalem to worship he came up with the not-so-bright idea of building his *own* altars all over the place so that the people of Israel could do their worshipping where they lived.

Just one difference.

Jeroboam had a golden calf idol made for each altar so that the Israelites could worship that instead of God.

Whoops! If you've read Boring Bible book *Magnificent Moses* you might remember that one of the special Ten Commandments that God gave the Israelites was...**don't worship idols!**

Not only did they build their own altars but they also built their own capital city called Samaria.

The people of Samaria were called Samaritans (bet you've heard **that** name before).

Boring Bible Fact: Jesus told a story about a man whom we call the Good Samaritan. It was all about how the people of Jerusalem hated the people of Samaria but how a Samaritan had decided to be kind to his enemy from the other city. This hatred began at the time of the split kingdoms.

All told, Israel, as the northern kingdom, managed to get through a staggering 19 *Catastrophic Kings* in their time.

Fascinating Fact:

Zimri takes the prize for being the king who lasted the shortest time. His reign was a measly 7 days! He went and killed himself by setting his palace on fire rather than be captured by his enemies.

One of the worst of the bunch was definitely King Ahab.
Ahab was a nasty piece of work but compared with his wife Jezebel he was an angel.

Ahab ruled for 22 disastrous years and added insult to injury by building a temple to the horrible god Baal so that Jezebel could worship there.
She wanted Baal to be Israel's main god.

Now, one thing to remember is this.
Although God was punishing his people for turning against him, his big plan was still to use them to show the rest of the world that he loved them and wanted to be their friend.
Although the Israelites had been unfaithful, God couldn't be.
It simply wasn't in his nature.
That's why he decided to send special messengers to the people of Israel to remind them that he was still alive and kicking and could still see everything they were getting up to - good or bad!

I'd like you to meet Elijah...

Elijah was going to start telling Ahab and the Israelites one or two things they probably didn't want to hear.
And to prove it was God that had sent him, God had given Elijah the power to do some amazing miracles.

The proper name for someone like Elijah is a '**prophet**'.

No, not profit. **Prophet!**
Being a prophet wasn't a job you'd choose.
You didn't usually win too many friends with your messages of doom and gloom.

ELIJAH'S DAILY DIARY

DEAR DIARY

Today has been quite an eventful day.
Was planning to do a spot of gardening when God gave me a message for King Ahab.
It's always a bit scary going to the palace especially when Jezebel's about.
I successfully managed to avoid that old witch and gave King Ahab the message.
*I told him that the Lord, the living God of Israel, says that there won't be any rain or dew for the next two or three years until **I** say so.*
That was it. I don't think Ahab liked what I said but fortunately God had already warned me to do a runner which is why I'm writing this miles from home by the brook of Cherith.

DEAR DIARY

Feeling a bit peckish.
Didn't think to bring a packed lunch.
Luckily for me, God has already sorted my menu.
Every day the ravens drop by to deliver bread and meat like God's told them to do.
A nice swig of brook water washes it all down nicely.

DEAR DIARY

Because there's no rain the brook has dried up.
***Now** what am I going to do?*

DEAR DIARY

All's well!
God told me to go to Zarephath.
He's arranged for a widow to feed me.
It'll make a change from ravens.

DEAR DIARY

I found the widow that God said and asked her for food and water.
Would you believe it?
She only had enough olive oil and flour for one last meal for herself and her son and then that was it. Not to worry, all was not lost.
We shared the food and then God gave me some good news for her.
I told her that her bowl wouldn't run out of flour or her jar run out of oil until God sent rain again. And just in case you're wondering - it didn't!

DEAR DIARY

The widow's son has been ill for a while.
Today he got worse and died.
His mother was grief-stricken.
But I took the boy upstairs, stretched myself out on him three times and prayed to God.
Praise the living God!
He brought the child back to life!
What a celebration we had, I can tell you.

DEAR DIARY

Today I had a showdown with 450 prophets of Baal and 400 prophets of Asherah.
In full view of all the Israelites and King Ahab I challenged them to prove that their horrible gods were real.

They built an altar to their gods and I made one to my God.
The challenge was to get their god to burn up the bull they'd
sacrificed by getting Baal to send down fire on it.

They danced and shouted round the altar like lunatics all day
long but nothing happened.
I was a bit naughty and started taking the mickey out of them.
You'd have done the same, they looked so ridiculous!
When they'd given up I got ready for my turn. To make it harder
I soaked my altar in gallons of water and guess what? As soon as
I prayed to God fire came down from the sky and burned my
sacrifice to a frazzle.
The Israelites wasted no time in worshipping God instead of Baal.
Oh, yes. Just one more thing. We had all the other prophets
killed.
What a day!

DEAR DIARY

Have had to do another runner!
When Jezebel found out what I'd done she wanted to have my
guts for garters. When I couldn't run any more I crashed out
under a tree and slept. God sent an angel to wake me up and
feed me so I'd have the strength to keep going.

DEAR DIARY

Today I met Elisha.
He's going to be my second-in-command.
You'd think he'd have a name that couldn't be confused with
mine, wouldn't you?

DEAR DIARY

Today King Ahab died a pretty ghastly death.
A nasty end to a nasty person, that's what I say.

DEAR DIARY

I somehow get the feeling that this will be the last time I write anything.

I've got to go out for a bit and Elisha insists on coming with me. He's persistent, I'll give him that!

HI, DIARY, ELISHA HERE!

I'm afraid Elijah won't be writing any more. As I stood and watched, an amazing chariot of fire pulled by horses of fire came down from heaven and took Elijah to be with God.

What a man he must have been for God not even to allow him to die first. That's all. Over and out for the last time!

There were only two people that the Bible tells us ever went to heaven without dying. Elijah was one and the other was a man called Enoch who is mentioned in Boring Bible book *Ballistic Beginnings.*

Just to let you know, Elisha also did some amazing things in his time (in God's power), like making an axe-head float, making a jar of oil so it never got empty and bringing a boy back to life. But I'm afraid you'll have to check those stories out in a real Bible.

Israel, the northern kingdom, lasted about 200 years until it was attacked and conquered by the Assyrians.

Sad to say, the Israelites were taken back to Assyria as prisoners. Time and time again, God had warned the Israelites to turn from their wicked ways but they had stubbornly refused to listen.

Now, at long last they paid the highest price.

They were taken from the land that God had given them.

THE SOUTHERN KINGDOM

Just like the Israelites in the north, the kingdom of Judah also had nineteen kings but they also had one queen, Athaliah.
The history of Judah was a little bit better than that of Israel but not much.
When the land first split into two kingdoms, a lot of the people from up north came to live in Judah so that they could still worship God in the Temple at Jerusalem.
Perhaps having the Temple there helped keep some of them on track but loads of others went off the rails.
The Bible says that they wasted no time in building altars to all the false gods of the surrounding nations.
By rejecting God they were also removing his hand of protection.
That meant the Egyptians were able to successfully attack Jerusalem and carry off all the wonderful treasures from the Temple.

It wasn't **all** bad.

Judah did have **some** good kings who tried to please God...

Judah's Good Guys

King Asa

He got rid of all the idols and their places of worship.

He also removed his grandmother, Maacah, from her position as queen mother because she worshipped the goddess Asherah.

King Jehoshaphat

He was Asa's son and he cleared out anything and everything to do with foreign gods. Jehoshaphat also made peace with Israel!

King Joash

He sort of did what was right in God's eyes but only because he had Jehoida the priest to keep prompting him. One good thing Joash did was make sure the Temple got repaired.

King Amaziah

King Amaziah also tried his best to please God but like his dad, Joash, he didn't actually get rid of the places of worship to idols.

King Uzziah

Likewise, Uzziah went half way to pleasing God but because he still allowed sacrifices to be made to idols God struck him down with a terrible skin disease.

King Jotham, King Josiah and King Hezekiah were also kings who in some way pleased God but Hezekiah beat the rest of them hands down for being obedient to God.

King Hezekiah

The Bible says that Judah never had another king quite like Hezekiah. Not only did he follow all God's commands but he got rid of all the places of worship to idols throughout Judah.

When Jerusalem was under siege from the taunting and terrible Assyrian army, God sent an angel and wiped out 185,000 Assyrian soldiers without Hezekiah's men having to lift a finger.

And another time, when Hezekiah was about to die, God agreed to his request to heal him. (In fact, the Bible says that God gave Hezekiah an extra fifteen years of life.)

God gave Hezekiah an awesome sign that he would do exactly what he'd promised by making the shadow of the sun actually go back about 40 minutes or so on the sundial!

Despite all that, the kingdom of Judah never really stayed loyal to God for long.

Although the southern kingdom lasted for around 300 years they eventually ended up going the same way as the northern kingdom.

King Nebuchadnezzar of Babylon came up with all his vast army and conquered the people of Judah and took them away to Babylon as prisoners.

Now here's something for you to do.

Go and ask your mum and dad (or any adult for that matter) if they remember a pop group called 'Bony M'?

If they do they'll probably also recall that 'Bony M' sang a song about 'the rivers of babylon, where we sat down and wept and remembered Zion'. Well, for your info, that was a song (taken from the Bible) all about God's people exiled in Babylon and crying every time they thought about Jerusalem (or Zion).

Fascinating Fact:

Archaeologists have discovered stone tablets that tell of the attack on Jerusalem from Nebuchadnezzar's viewpoint. Unsurprisingly, it is very similar to the account of events recorded in the Bible.

Just in case you're wondering why God didn't send any prophets to the southern kingdom let me put the record straight and tell you about a handful of them, just before we leave the people of Judah for good.

First there was **Isaiah.**
Isaiah was a prophet during Hezekiah's reign.
Not only did Isaiah warn the people of Judah what would happen if they disobeyed God but he also gave them an idea what would happen *after* their punishment.
But the best bit of what Isaiah said was the stuff about Jesus.
If you want to find out what sort of things Isaiah said about Jesus then I'm afraid you're going to have to buy a copy of the next Boring Bible book in this series called *Super Son*.

Boring Bible Fact: There is a whole book called 'Isaiah' in the Bible which tells us a lot of the things Isaiah said. It is divided into two parts, the first part having 39 chapters and the second part having 27 chapters. Amazingly that's exactly how the Bible is divided up. There are 39 books in the Old Testament and 27 books in the New Testament!

**Boring Bible Joke: Why couldn't Isaiah wear glasses?
Because one EYE'S 'IGHER than the other!**

Then there was **Jeremiah**.

Jeremiah not only warned the southern kingdom to 'get back to God or a foreign army would attack them' but he ended up getting carted off with them to Babylon as a prisoner.

Jeremiah was nicknamed the 'Weeping Prophet' because that's what he seemed to spend a lot of time doing.

Daniel (you might have heard of his night in a lions' den) was a young man when he was taken captive to Babylon.

God gave Daniel the ability to interpret dreams (like Joseph in Boring Bible book *Hotchpotch Hebrews*).

God used Daniel to influence the Babylonian kings and to show them who God was.

Chapter Two - That's All Folks!

God had promised the Jewish people (that's another name for the Israelites) that one day they would return to their land.

The Bible tells us that's exactly what happened but the place they came back to 70 years later was in ruins.

They did manage to rebuild the Temple but it was never quite as magnificent as in Solomon's time.

And while they'd been in exile, other people had moved in which made things a lot tougher.

The Jews who came back from exile in Babylon returned with one or two new ideas.

Because they couldn't worship God in the Temple while they were in exile, they built lots of smaller buildings called synagogues, which are a bit like churches.

One last thing.

Over time, many of the Jewish people forgot how to speak the Hebrew language and took to speaking Greek because the Greek empire had reached their doorstep.

The next book in this series, as we've already said, is *Super Son*. From the last prophet, Malachi, until the time of Jesus' birth, there was nobody to speak for God in all of Israel.

For 400 long years God would be completely silent as far as they were concerned.

The next prophet to show his face would herald the arrival of the final piece in the jigsaw of God's brilliant plan to restore his friendship with the human race.

Malachi, the last of these prophets, leaves the Jewish nation with a promise to hold on to, that one day, in the future, God will once more return to his Temple.

But will he appear as an awesome cloud of shining light in whose presence nobody can stand or will he appear in a way that nobody was expecting?

To find out, you'll just have to read *Super Son*.

The Bit at the End

Here's a few reminders of some of the stuff we've looked at in *Catastrophic Kings*.

What's Been Happening

Joshua and Israelites enter Canaan (at last!).
Lots and lots of battles (including Jericho).
Joshua dies.
Judges come and go (Samson gets a haircut!).
Israelites demand a king.
Saul rules.
David becomes a ruler (not the twelve inch sort!).
Solomon makes some wise moves.
Israel splits.
Lots and lots of kings (and some prophets).
Israel's downfall.
God promises to come back one day...

A Quick Run-Down Of The Main Characters

Joshua.
Ehud (kills Eglon with a thud!).
Deborah.

Gideon.

Samson.

Samuel (the kingmaker).

Saul.

David (shepherd, harpist and king).

Solomon.

So many kings there's not enough room to mention them!

Elijah (and Elisha).

Isaiah, Jeremiah and Daniel.

And God (obviously!).

Your Turn

Write down any bits of the Bible that you don't think are quite so boring any more.

Don't forget to get your hands on a copy of a proper Bible so you can check out loads of the stuff we didn't even have room for in this book.

Nowadays lots of Bibles are written in modern language so you don't have to worry about not being able to understand the words they use.

Enjoy yourself!